# LADY GAGA
## Making a Difference as a Musician

By Katie Kawa

KidHaven
PUBLISHING

People Who Make a Difference

Published in 2021 by
**KidHaven Publishing, an Imprint of Greenhaven Publishing, LLC**
353 3rd Avenue
Suite 255
New York, NY 10010

Designer: Deanna Paternostro
Editor: Katie Kawa

Photo credits: Cover Kevin Mazur/Getty Images for Park MGM Las Vegas; p. 5 George Pimentel/Getty Images for TIFF; p. 7 Kevin Mazur/Getty Images; p. 9 (main) JStone/Shutterstock.com; p. 9 (inset) Jay Directo/AFP/GettyImages; p. 10 FAGRI/Shutterstock.com; p. 11 Rommel Demano/FilmMagic/Getty Images; p. 13 Desiree Navarro/WireImage/Getty Images; p. 15 Ronald Martinez/Getty Images; p. 17 (main) Tinseltown/Shutterstock.com; p. 17 (inset) Jerod Harris/FilmMagic/Getty Images; p. 19 Neilson Barnard/Getty Images for ELLE Magazine; p. 20 Kevin Mazur/Getty Images for Haus Laboratories; p. 21 T.Sumaetho/Shutterstock.com.

**Library of Congress Cataloging-in-Publication Data**

Names: Kawa, Katie, author.
Title: Lady Gaga : making a difference as a musician / Katie Kawa.
Description: [First edition.] | New York : KidHaven Publishing, 2021. |
    Series: People who make a difference | Includes index.
Identifiers: LCCN 2019060005 (print) | LCCN 2019060006 (ebook) | ISBN
    9781534534780 (library binding) | ISBN 9781534534766 (paperback) | ISBN
    9781534534773 (set) | ISBN 9781534534797 (ebook)
Subjects: LCSH: Lady Gaga–Juvenile literature. | Singers–United
    States–Biography–Juvenile literature.
Classification: LCC ML3930.L13 K38 2021  (print) | LCC ML3930.L13  (ebook)
    | DDC 782.42164092 [B]–dc23
LC record available at https://lccn.loc.gov/2019060005
LC ebook record available at https://lccn.loc.gov/2019060006

Printed in the United States of America

Some of the images in this book illustrate individuals who are models. The depictions do not imply actual situations or events.

CPSIA compliance information: Batch #BS20K: For further information contact Greenhaven Publishing LLC, New York, New York at 1-844-317-7404.

Please visit our website, www.greenhavenpublishing.com. For a free color catalog of all our high-quality books, call toll free 1-844-317-7404 or fax 1-844-317-7405.

Find us on

# CONTENTS

# THE POWER OF MUSIC

Music can do many things. It can make people happy. It can remind them of important moments in their lives and people they love. It can also inspire people, making them believe they can do something great.

Lady Gaga's music has inspired people around the world. It's helped many people feel proud to be themselves and feel seen and accepted for exactly who they are. Lady Gaga grew up wanting to make a difference in the world, and her music is just one way she's doing that. She's using her voice to make the world a better and kinder place.

## In Her Words

"I recognized very early on that my impact was to help liberate [free] people through kindness."

— Interview with Oprah Winfrey for *Elle* magazine from November 2019

Lady Gaga became famous for her music—and her wild style—but she's now also known as an actress and an activist, or a person who fights for causes she cares about.

# BIG DREAMS AND BULLIES

Lady Gaga's real name is Stefani Joanne Angelina Germanotta. She was born on March 28, 1986, and grew up in New York City. Stefani loved music, and she started playing the piano at a very young age. By the time she was a teenager, she was already writing her own songs!

Music helped Stefani get through hard times while she was growing up. She was bullied in school, and writing songs helped her deal with her feelings of not being good enough. Today, her music helps a lot of other young people who are being bullied too.

## In Her Words

"Sometimes, it's hard to stand up against the popular kids … and hang out with someone who's being bullied, but be the bigger person. Be kinder. Be braver."

— Instagram video from October 2017

Lady Gaga grew up with a lot of love and support from her family. She's still very close with her mother, Cynthia, her sister, Natali, and her father, Joe.

# MOTHER MONSTER

Stefani didn't let bullies stop her from dreaming big and working hard to make her dreams come true. She took voice lessons, dance lessons, and acting lessons. She sang at clubs around New York City and began using the name Lady Gaga.

At first, Lady Gaga wrote songs for other singers, but in 2008, her album, *The Fame*, became a big hit. The next year, her second album, *The Fame Monster*, earned her even more fans. These fans, who call themselves Little Monsters, like that Lady Gaga looks and sounds different from anyone else. She inspires them to love the things that make them **unique**!

### In Her Words

"You know, I didn't use to be brave. In fact I wasn't very brave at all, but you have made me brave, Little Monsters … I would dream that someday, one person would believe in me. So when you leave here tonight, know that at least one person believes in you."

— Speech given during The Monster Ball tour, which ran from 2009 to 2011

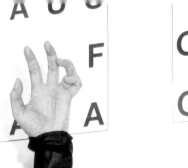

HAUS OF GAGA

NSGAGA UNS

Lady Gaga's fans often call her Mother Monster, and she shares inspiring messages with them on **social media** and during her live shows and tours. Another way she shows her fans she cares is by putting her "paws up," as shown here, which is a sign that connects Little Monsters around the world.

# "BORN THIS WAY"

In 2011, Lady Gaga put out her third album, *Born This Way*. The first song she **released** from this album had the same title. This song didn't just become a huge hit, it also made a difference in many people's lives.

"Born This Way" is a song about being proud of who you are. In this song, Lady Gaga sings that people of all races, genders, and backgrounds should see themselves as beautiful. This song was especially important for members of the **LGBT+ community**. "Born This Way" became an **anthem** for this community, which is very close to Lady Gaga's heart.

## In Her Words

I'm beautiful in my way
'Cause God makes no mistakes
I'm on the right track, baby
I was born this way

— "Born This Way"

Many members of the LGBT+ community found comfort and acceptance in the message of "Born This Way," which is that people should be accepted for who they are. Lady Gaga continues to use her voice to fight for this community, especially their right to marriage equality.

# HELPING YOUNG PEOPLE

The message behind "Born This Way" was also shown in many other things Lady Gaga did after that song and album came out. For example, in 2012, Lady Gaga and her mother helped create the Born This Way Foundation. This is an organization, or group, that works to support young people's **mental** and **emotional** health.

The year after the Born This Way Foundation was created, the Born Brave Bus became part of Lady Gaga's Born This Way Ball tour. The bus was part of an effort by Lady Gaga to give her fans **access** to mental health services and ways to help their communities.

## In Her Words

"You know, it's very easy to say to someone, 'Be brave,' but it's not so easy to practice … But give yourself time. Allow yourself to take little bites every day. That's what I would say: Take little bites of bravery."

— Interview with Oprah Winfrey for *Elle* magazine from November 2019

The Born Brave Bus was created to give young people
a safe space to talk about their feelings and their problems.

# MORE MUSIC

While working to help young people through the Born This Way Foundation, Lady Gaga also continued to make music. Her album *ARTPOP* came out in 2013, but the next year, Lady Gaga did something very different. She took a break from her wild fashion choices and pop hits to record a jazz album with a singer named Tony Bennett, who's been famous for many years.

Lady Gaga returned to pop music in 2016 with her album *Joanne*. It was named after her aunt, who died at a young age. Each of these albums allowed Lady Gaga to reach new groups of fans.

## In Her Words

"As much as we all love the fashion and the makeup and the glamour, this isn't a beauty **pageant**. It's about the heart and the drive and the work. Of course, it's lovely to dress up and **compliment** one another and feel good—but that shouldn't be the very first thing."

— Interview with *Glamour* magazine from August 2017

Lady Gaga sang at the Super Bowl in 2017. That year, a movie about her life—*Gaga: Five Foot Two*—came out that showed the hard work that went into getting ready for the Super Bowl. The movie also gave fans a closer look into Lady Gaga's life.

# ACTING IN A *STAR IS BORN*

When Lady Gaga was a girl growing up in New York City, her first dream wasn't to be a singer—it was to be an actress. However, it wasn't until 2018 that she starred in her first major movie. That year, she played the character of Ally in *A Star Is Born*. She also wrote and sang many songs in the movie, including the hit song "Shallow."

*A Star Is Born* deals with mental health issues, and Lady Gaga has often talked about the importance of being open about these issues. She wants people dealing with mental health problems to know that it's okay to ask for help.

## In Her Words

"I'm so proud to be a part of a movie that addresses mental health issues … They're so important. And a lot of artists deal with that, and we've got to take care of each other. So if you see somebody that's hurting, don't look away. And if you're hurting, even though it might be hard, try to find that bravery within yourself to dive deep and go tell somebody."

— Speech at the 2019 Grammy Awards

**2019 Grammy Awards**

Lady Gaga won many awards, or prizes, for acting in *A Star Is Born* and for writing "Shallow." This included a Grammy Award, which is the most famous award a musician can win, and an Academy Award—also called an Oscar—which is the most famous award in the movie business.

**2019 Oscars**

17

# RAISING AWARENESS

As Lady Gaga talked about mental health awareness in *A Star Is Born*, she also talked about her own struggles with mental health. She's been open about dealing with trauma, which is an upsetting experience that can cause lasting mental health problems. She's lived with **depression** and **anxiety**, and she's talked about these issues because she hopes that she can help other people dealing with them know they're not alone.

Lady Gaga has also raised awareness about chronic pain disorders—conditions that cause pain that doesn't go away. She lives with one of these disorders and is working to educate others about them.

### In Her Words

"Depression, anxiety, … trauma—these are just a few examples of the [things] that can lead to this … pain. So what I would like to say in this room of powerful women and men today is let's work together to beckon [call] the world towards kindness… I want to see mental health become a global [worldwide] **priority**."

— Speech at the *Elle* Women in Hollywood event in October 2018

# The Life of Lady Gaga

**1986**
Stefani Joanne Angelina Germanotta is born in New York City.

**2008**
Lady Gaga's first album, *The Fame*, is released.

**2009**
*The Fame Monster* is released

**2011**
"Born This Way" becomes a hit, and the *Born This Way* album comes out.

**2012**
Lady Gaga creates the Born This Way Foundation with her mother.

**2013**
The Born Brave Bus begins touring with Lady Gaga.

*ARTPOP* is released.

**2014**
Lady Gaga releases *Cheek to Cheek*—an album of jazz songs with Tony Bennett.

**2016**
Lady Gaga releases the album *Joanne*.

**2017**
Lady Gaga sings at the Super Bowl.

*Gaga: Five Foot Two* comes out on Netflix.

**2018**
Lady Gaga stars in *A Star Is Born*.

**2019**
Lady Gaga wins a Grammy and an Oscar for "Shallow."

Lady Gaga creates a line of makeup called Haus Laboratories.

Lady Gaga has been famous for only a little more than 10 years. However, she's already made a huge difference in the worlds of music, movies, and much more!

# NEW WAYS TO MAKE A DIFFERENCE

Lady Gaga is still finding new ways to inspire people. In 2019, she created a line of makeup with her makeup artist Sarah Tanno-Stewart that's called Haus Laboratories. Lady Gaga has talked about how playing with makeup was a way for her to become more comfortable facing the world. She wants Haus Laboratories to help all people feel beautiful and powerful.

Helping people, especially through music, has always been important to Lady Gaga. She's also used her fame to raise money and awareness for causes she cares about. Lady Gaga was born to be a star—and born to make a difference!

### In Her Words

"If I'm not changing people's lives, what are we doing here?"

— Interview with *Allure* magazine from October 2019

# Be Like Lady Gaga!

Reach out to people who have been bullied, and work to stop bullying in your school.

Love yourself, and let your family and friends know they're loved for exactly who they are.

Speak out about issues that matter to you. Maybe you can write a song about them!

If someone you know is dealing with mental health issues, tell a trusted adult.

Be kind to people.

If you like to write songs, try writing songs with positive messages that make people feel included.

Learn more about issues such as mental health and bullying.

Work hard at whatever you love to do, whether it's playing music, sports, or writing.

Lady Gaga inspires many people to be braver, kinder, and more accepting of themselves and others. If her story has inspired you, here are just a few ways you can make a difference too!

# GLOSSARY

**access:** The ability to use or have something.

**anthem:** A song that is connected to or honors a certain group of people or way of thinking.

**anxiety:** A mental illness with signs that include a sense of fear that is too strong for a given situation or a feeling of worry that won't go away.

**compliment:** To say something nice about someone.

**depression:** A mental illness with signs that include sadness, hopelessness, and a lack of interest in doing things that were once considered enjoyable.

**emotional:** Relating to feelings.

**LGBT+ community:** A group made up of people who see themselves as a gender different from the sex they were assigned at birth or who want to be in romantic relationships that aren't only male-female. LGBT stands for lesbian, gay, bisexual, and transgender.

**mental:** Relating to the mind.

**pageant:** A contest that is often treated like a show.

**priority:** A condition of being more important than other things.

**release:** To make something available to the public.

**social media:** A collection of websites and applications, or apps, that allow users to interact with each other and create online communities.

**unique:** Special or different from anything else.

# FOR MORE INFORMATION

## WEBSITES

### *Billboard*: Lady Gaga

*www.billboard.com/music/lady-gaga*

*Billboard* magazine's website has news about Lady Gaga and a list of albums and songs she's released.

### Born This Way Foundation

*bornthisway.foundation*

The official website of the Born This Way Foundation offers facts about the work this organization does and ways you can get involved.

## BOOKS

Lacey, Jane. *Bullying*. New York, NY: PowerKids Press, 2019.

Lajiness, Kate. *Lady Gaga: Famous Entertainer*. Minneapolis, MN: ABDO Publishing, 2018.

Merwin, E. *Lady Gaga*. Minneapolis, MN: Bearport Publishing, 2019.

# INDEX

Stanly County Public Library
133 E Main St.
Albemarle, NC 28001